Bowhill Colliery, Cardenden, Fife, in 1917. Loaded railway wagons are emerging from under the screens.

COAL MINING

Geoffrey Hayes

Shire Publications

Contents

Cover photograph: *Winding headgears over the shafts at the former Woodhorn Colliery, Ashington, Northumberland, now the Woodhorn Colliery Museum. The far shaft was the 'upcast', and the enclosure around the headgear is the airlock that prevented short-circuiting of the ventilation air current.*

ACKNOWLEDGEMENTS
I acknowledge the assistance given by the Lancashire Mining Museum and the Scottish Mining Museum in the preparation of this book, and also the invaluable first-hand information imparted by the late James W. Houston. My wife, Naomi, provided a great deal of help by reading the script and providing critical analysis.
Illustrations are acknowledged as follows: from *Coal Mining Practice* (Caxton, 1959), pages 10 (centre), 19 (centre), 25 (top); Cadbury Lamb, front cover; Lancashire Mining Museum, page 15 (top); Lancashire Mining Museum/Coal Authority, page 15 (bottom); Lancashire Mining Museum/Tony France, pages 9 (bottom), 11 (top), 11 (centre), 17 (bottom), 18 (top), 29, 31; Lancashire Mining Museum/Mrs White, page 4 (top); John Ryan collection, copyright J. A. Peden, pages 1, 8 (top), 14 (bottom), 27 (top), 27 (centre). Other photographs and drawings are by the author or from his collection.

British Library Cataloguing in Publication Data: Hayes, G. (Geoffrey), 1932- Coal mining. – (Shire album; 349) 1. Coal-mining machinery – Great Britain – History 2. Coal mines and mining – Great Britain – History I. Title 622.3'34'0941 ISBN 0 7478 0434 6.

Published in 2000 by Shire Publications Ltd, Cromwell House, Church Street, Princes Risborough, Buckinghamshire HP27 9AA, UK. (Website: www.shirebooks.co.uk)
Copyright © 2000 by Geoffrey Hayes. First published 2000. Shire Album 349. ISBN 0 7478 0434 6.
Geoffrey Hayes is hereby identified as the author of this work in accordance with Section 77 of the Copyright, Designs and Patents Act 1988.

Printed in Great Britain by CIT Printing Services Ltd, Press Buildings, Merlins Bridge, Haverfordwest, Pembrokeshire SA61 1XF.

A representation of an early-nineteenth-century mine at Summerlee Heritage Park, Coatbridge, Lanarkshire. The winding engine is the original Newcomen-type engine of 1810 from Ferme Colliery, Rutherglen.

Introduction

The rocks forming the earth's crust underneath the British Isles have been rich in valuable minerals. Copper, tin, lead, zinc, iron and even gold, as well as coal, have all been extensively mined. Usually they have been difficult and dangerous to extract. The discovery of more easily worked deposits overseas has caused the decline of all mining in the British Isles.

Coal mining in Britain is an old occupation. The Romans worked coal seams that had come to the surface as outcrops, and possibly there was some working before then. Monks in Scotland were mining coal in the thirteenth century. In past years the demand for coal was so great that it was worked wherever it was found. Today it may seem almost inconceivable that there were coal mines in Sutherland, on the Mull of Kintyre and in Ireland. The largely rural counties of Somerset, Gloucestershire and Kent had their coal mines too.

The major coalfields were in the central belt across Scotland, in north-west and north-east England, in the English midland counties of Staffordshire, Derbyshire and Nottinghamshire, and in South Wales from Monmouthshire in the east to Pembrokeshire in the west. There were also smaller but nevertheless important

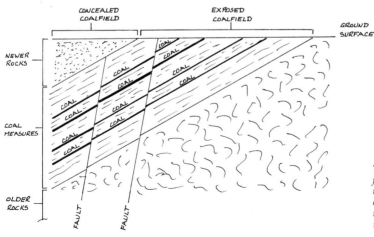

The typical formation of coal measures and their coal seams between newer and older rock beds.

James Roscoe & Sons' New Lester Colliery, Tyldesley, Lancashire, c.1940, near the end of its working life. On the left is the 'jig' coal washer with a cone for separating fine dirt particles from the wash water.

coalfields in Leicestershire, Warwickshire, Shropshire and North Wales in addition to the rural counties mentioned above.

The north-east coalfields in Durham and Northumberland were the first to achieve high production as they had access to London by sea and river for their coal. Other coalfields were restricted to local needs by lack of transport until the building of canals and railways. There were soon hundreds of coal trains making the journey from Nottinghamshire, Derbyshire and South Wales to London. Trains also carried coal from the coalfields in Scotland, South Wales and north-west and north-east England to the ports to fulfil huge export orders and fuel ships. In addition coal was needed in local factories and ironworks. Coal production reached 287 million tons in 1913. When the First World War broke out in 1914 coal exports ceased almost overnight and were never to return to their pre-war levels.

After the war, a worldwide trade depression wreaked havoc with the coal-mining industry. From the 1913 peak, annual output declined and continued to do so for most years after 1918. Many coalfields were already becoming worked out and mines were also facing increasing costs because of water, geological problems and thin seams. As an example, the Lancashire and Cheshire coalfield achieved peak production of 26.5 million tons in 1907. By 1930 production was down to 15 million tons and in 1935 mining ceased in the Cheshire coalfield.

Until 1947 coal mines in Britain were privately owned and the industry was fragmented in spite of an Act of Parliament in 1926 which encouraged amalgamations of companies. In 1947 all mines, except very small ones, were nationalised. An

enormous amount of investment followed but in the end failed to halt the decline in the industry. During the 1990s the few remaining mines returned to private ownership. Coal mining today is concentrated in Nottinghamshire and Yorkshire, where the geological conditions are generally more favourable than elsewhere.

Caphouse Colliery, near Wakefield, West Yorkshire, which closed in 1979. It is now the National Coal Mining Museum for England. Most of the headgear is of timber construction. The winding engine is a twin-cylinder horizontal, built in 1876.

Winning the coal

The land which forms most of the British Isles once had a tropical climate. Coal seams are buried tropical forests. These forests grew in the Carboniferous period of the Palaeozoic era, when plants and animals that left the first fossils emerged. Inundation by the sea buried the forests under sand and mud, which eventually became rock. Later there were massive upheavals of the earth's crust, which, together with subsequent erosion by wind and rain, brought the rocks containing the coal seams (the 'Coal Measures') near to the surface, where they were visible as outcrops. The upheavals also caused huge fractures in the rocks (faults) and in places volcanic necks burst through, burning the coal nearby to cinder.

SHAFTS AND DRIFTS

At first coal was worked where it was visible at the surface or just below thin deposits of soil. When simple digging became impossible, shallow shafts were sunk and the coal was extracted around the bottom of the hole. These were known as 'bell pits' because the excavation was shaped like a bell. When collapse was imminent, another shaft was sunk nearby. Early mine shafts or pits were variously shaped: round, oval, rectangular and square. Round shafts lined in brickwork were the most used as this shape was the strongest, although in Scotland square shafts lined in timber were often favoured. Some of these timber-lined shafts lasted to the middle of the twentieth century. The most modern shafts are concrete-lined as this is a most effective method of keeping out water. Before concrete technology had developed, cast-iron sections ('tubbing') were used to line shafts where they passed through unstable and waterlogged ground.

Modern mine shafts are about 25 feet (7.6 metres) in diameter. There has been a gradual increase in size from early shafts, which could be as small as 4 feet (1.2 metres) in diameter. Shaft depths varied greatly. Old shafts were usually shallower than later ones but this was not always the case. Pendleton Colliery near Manchester was producing 1000 tons a day in 1843. The two shafts, both 8 feet (2.4 metres) in diameter, were 525 yards (480 metres) deep. By contrast New Lount in Leicestershire, sunk in 1924, was 100 yards (91 metres) deep. Parsonage Colliery in Lancashire, completed in 1920, had two shafts of 1008 yards (922 metres). During the 1950s several new shafts were sunk and some old ones were deepened to reach further reserves. Wolstanton Colliery in North Staffordshire was deepened to 1150 yards (1052 metres).

Sinking deep shafts to reach coal seams has always been a long and difficult

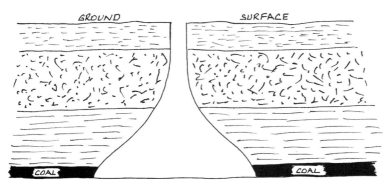

A 'bell pit' in section.

5

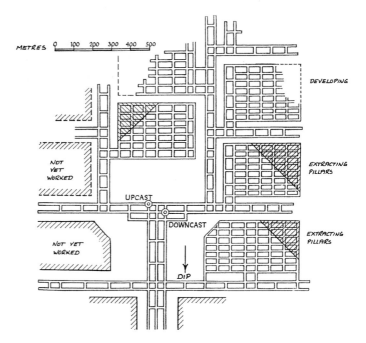

The layout of bord and pillar workings. In the early days of coal mining the pillars of coal were left behind. As knowledge improved, the pillars were extracted as the miners retreated from the area, leaving a worked-out 'waste', shown shaded in the diagram.

operation, and water was often a problem. Some sinkings had to be abandoned because the quantity of water flowing in was too great to be pumped out. During the twentieth century the practice of freezing the ground, and with it the water, was often adopted. Large refrigeration plants were built to cool brine below the freezing point of water. The brine was injected into the ground to form an 'ice wall' around the shaft. Sinking could then proceed as if in dry ground. When the shaft was complete, the freezing plant was dismantled and the ground returned to normal.

As the shafts are such vital parts of a mine, they have to be protected from ground movement and a 'pillar' of unworked coal is always left around them. Even this did not prevent some shafts from collapsing. Since 1862 all mines have had to have two linked shafts to allow for escape.

Sometimes coal seams were visible in the sides of valleys and cliffs, into which the old miners drove small tunnels ('headings') narrow enough to be self-supporting. When the air became too foul to breathe, another heading was started. A great deal of coal was left and, as miners became bolder, they dug cross tunnels or headings to connect the previous headings in order to extract more coal. Thus came into being a method of working known variously as 'pillar and stall', 'stoop and room', or 'bord and pillar'. This method was also used to win or mine the coal from the bottom of shafts, with the miners working outwards through the coal seam. Pillars of coal were left to hold up the roof but, as knowledge improved, the coal pillars were reduced in size or removed altogether in a systematic retreat from the area. Mechanised bord and pillar working, with the pillars being completely extracted, was still used in some coalfields into the 1960s. As depths of working increased, the coal pillars crushed, which made bord and pillar unsuitable for deep seams. It was also unsuitable for seams less than 4 feet (1.2 metres) thick as coal transport ('haulage') roads then had to be cut partly into the roof or floor to allow ponies and, later in more modern times, mechanical transport to pass. Furthermore, there was nowhere to dispose of the stone ('dirt') underground.

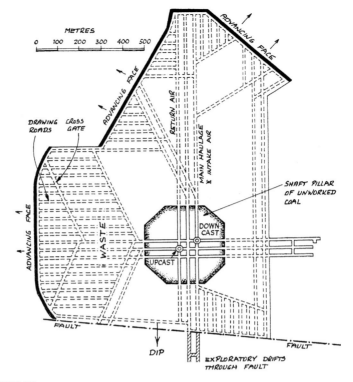

The layout of hand-got longwall face workings. It was common practice for these workings to spread out like a fan from the shafts, leaving an unworked 'pillar' around the shafts to protect them. Several seams at different depths would be worked simultaneously in this fashion.

LONGWALL WORKING

The 'longwall face' method of working is known to have been in use in Leicestershire by about 1625. Two 'gates' or subsidiary tunnels were driven off the main haulage road for a short distance. A heading was driven through the coal to connect them and when completed one side of the heading was advanced as a whole. Full production was quickly attained. The area left behind was known as the 'waste', 'goaf' or 'gob'. Temporary supports of timber props were used at the face itself and 'packs' of fallen stone were built in the waste as permanent roof support. The gates could be made big enough for ponies, and any stone was usefully disposed of in the waste. 'Drawing roads' for tubs or more primitive conveyances were made at intervals through the waste to serve the working places at the coal face.

Coal getting, as it was known, on a longwall face could be dangerous. Miners had to cut a deep slot ('hole out') under the coal seam. A combination of roof weight, picks, iron bars and, where necessary, explosives was then used to bring down the coal ready for shovelling into tubs. Although 'sprags' (short wooden props) were used to hold up the coal during holing out, falls of coal were frequent, causing injury and death.

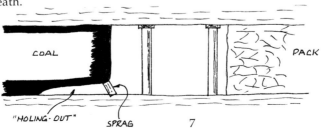

'Holing out' on a hand-got longwall face. The miner would hole out with his pick to a depth of about 6 feet (1.8 metres), working his way under the coal.

7

Miners working at the coalface of a thick seam at a colliery in the Wigan district, c.1900. The deputy or 'fireman', as he was still often called, is testing for firedamp near the roof, where it is likely to accumulate. Note the lack of protective headgear. Safety helmets eventually became mandatory.

MECHANISATION

With the introduction of compressed air power in collieries from about 1870, engineers began to look at ways of coal getting by machine. A relatively early success was the percussive coal cutter, which became widely used in coal headings and bord and pillar work. It was light enough to be carried and could be operated by two men. In operation it was similar to a dentist's drill, cutting slots in the coal as the miners did with their picks. Because of the length of its working face longwall working was more of a problem. Early coal cutters had a large disc carrying a great number of small picks. The machine travelled along the coalface cutting a slot, emulating the action of the miner's pick. Real success was not achieved until a machine was developed that carried the picks on an endless chain running around a 'jib' and driven by a compressed air turbine. Equally important was the use of face conveyors which transported the coal to the gate, where it was loaded into tubs. After cutting, the coal was blasted down with explosives and shovelled on to the conveyor. As the coal was cleared away the miners set props to support the roof. When the coal was completely cleared, some miners moved the conveyor forward whilst others extended the packs, removing props ('drawing off') as the packs were completed. Coalface work was still very labour-intensive.

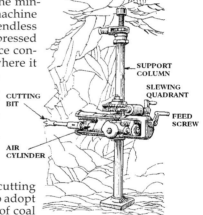

It was not until the 1930s that machine coal cutting began to develop but some coalfields were slow to adopt it. In the Manchester coalfields only 17 per cent of coal

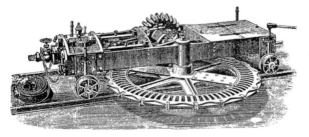

Above: *A percussive coal-cutting machine driven by compressed air for coal headings and much used in bord and pillar workings.*

Left: *A disc coal-cutting machine powered by compressed air, made by J. Scarisbrick Walker of Wigan in 1869.*

8

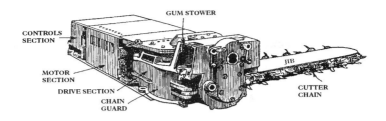

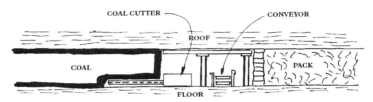

Above: *A jib and chain coal-cutting machine for electric motor or compressed-air turbine drive. The gum stower throws the fine cuttings on to the face conveyor.*

Above: *Section of machine-cut hand-loading longwall face. The coal is about 2 feet 8 inches (800 mm) thick.*

produced was cut by machine in 1930; an aggressive policy by a new company raised this to 98 per cent in 1946. These figures are remarkable when compared with the national averages of 31 and 74 per cent respectively over the same period. After 1945 a determined effort was made by engineers to develop 'cutter-loader' machines which, as the name implies, could cut the coal and also load it on to the face conveyor. They were helped by the widespread introduction of electrical power, which meant that coalface machinery could be much more powerful.

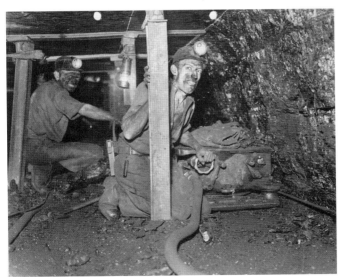

Coal cutting on a machine-cut, hand-loading coalface at Bedford Colliery, Lancashire, c.1940. The coal-cutting machine is an AB15, 15 inches (381 mm) high, made by Anderson, Boyes. The machine hauled itself along the coalface by the steel wire rope. Steel wedge props and 'W' steel roof bars are in use as supports. The miners are wearing battery electric safety cap lamps.

9

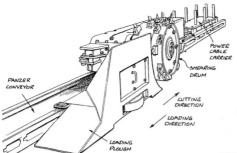

PANZER
CONVEYOR

POWER
CABLE
CARRIER

SHEARING
DRUM

CUTTING
DIRECTION

LOADING
DIRECTION

LOADING
PLOUGH

Left: An Anderton Shearer cutter-loader machine. During the cutting or shearing run, the machine tows the plough. Some coal falls on to the plough and is deflected on to the conveyor. At the end of the shearing run, the machine is reversed to push the plough, which scoops the remaining cut coal on to the conveyor. The machines were usually electrically driven, but a few had compressed-air turbines for use in very gassy seams. The latest machines have a shearer drum at both ends so that coal can be cut in both directions of travel.

Right: A Huwood slicer-loader machine and 'panzer' conveyor. The machine sliced the coal off the face and was successful where the coal readily broke off. The roof supports are German-made friction props. Water is being infused into the coalface to reduce the formation of dust.

Below: As the coal is extracted in longwall working, the roof above the seam is ripped (brought down) at the end of the gates in order to extend them. The gateside pack supports the edge of the exposed roof of the extracted seam alongside the gate behind the lagging of the steel arches. (See also top illustration on page 11.)

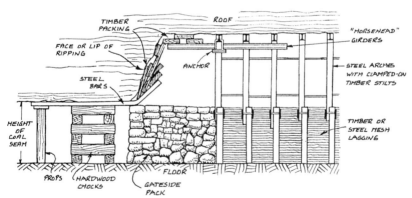

TIMBER PACKING

ROOF

FACE OR LIP OF RIPPING

ANCHOR

STEEL BARS

HEIGHT OF COAL SEAM

FLOOR

PROPS

HARDWOOD CHOCKS

GATESIDE PACK

"HORSEHEAD" GIRDERS

STEEL ARCHES WITH CLAMPED-ON TIMBER STILTS

TIMBER OR STEEL MESH LAGGING

The cutter-loader machines that became widely used ran on top of a heavy-duty steel conveyor, dubbed a 'panzer', which scraped the coal along a trough. When the machine had cut and loaded the coal, the conveyor could be snaked forward. Because the new machines were able to advance quickly, they outstripped the building of packs, which meant that potential production was not attained. This problem was eventually solved by the introduction on the coalfaces of very strong hydraulic roof supports instead of props. Where props yielded to some extent under the weight of the roof, causing it to bend downwards, the hydraulic supports remained firm. Instead of bending, the rocks forming the roof broke off and the waste was allowed to cave in completely. Packs were retained as permanent roof supports only alongside the gates to help protect them from crushing.

Right: *The end of a main gate serving a longwall face showing the 'rip' face or lip, steel arch supports with stilts and trough belt conveyor. The inclination of the coal seam is slight but noticeable. Bedford Colliery, Lancashire, c.1954.*

Left: *A main gate to a longwall coalface with trough belt conveyor and steel arch supports. The first effects of roof crush or 'weight' are becoming apparent. Ince Moss Colliery, Lancashire, 1938.*

Right: *Diagram showing a section of a horizon-mining system. Note the long, level tunnels and deep shafts which have to be driven and sunk before any mining commences.*

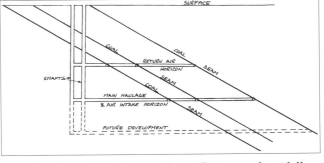

It was traditional in Britain for the main haulage and ventilation roads to follow inclined seams. As areas of coal were worked out, the roads were extended and new longwall faces were established. Development was a gradual process, as was the financial outlay that it involved. In Europe a system widely used was 'horizon mining'. Horizontal tunnels were driven at different levels ('horizons') from the shafts to intersect the inclined coal seams. At the intersections gates were driven and longwall faces commenced. Initial costs were high but the horizon tunnels were ideal for locomotive haulage as they were level. This system of mining was used in major mine developments in Britain after 1945, a high point in British coal mining. The confidence of that time has long gone but the system continues in use today.

Underground transport

For hundreds of years coal was transported from the working places to the shafts by human labour. Women, boys and girls were employed in this task. Coal was physically carried, dragged on sledges ('sleds'), hauled in baskets on trolleys, or brought by a combination of any of these methods. Following a government investigation in 1842, it became illegal to employ boys under ten and women and girls underground. Increasing demand for coal also required better means of transport. The 'tub',

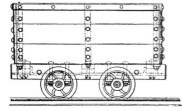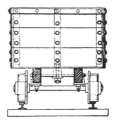

A nineteenth-century wooden coal tub. It is about 1.35 metres long. Later tubs were made of steel to prevent spillage of coal dust and minimise the risk of explosions.

'tram', 'dan' or 'hutch' (in Scotland) came into being; this was a small railway truck carrying 5 to 7 hundredweights (275 to 385 kg) of coal. Pit ponies were introduced to haul tubs but they could only be used where the roadways were fairly level and were high enough for them to pass. Boys and youths were still employed extensively to transport coal from the working places to the pony haulage road.

As most coal seams are inclined, self-acting inclines ('jigs') were introduced, whereby descending 'fulls' hauled up ascending

Above: *An old wooden 'tub' or 'hutch' preserved by the entrance to Castlebridge Colliery, Clackmannan.*

Right: *The entrance to the main underground water level of the Duke of Bridgewater's collieries at Worsley, Lancashire. Construction began in 1759 and eventually there were 46 miles (74 km) of underground waterways transporting coal and draining the workings. Iron-stained water was still issuing in 1999.*

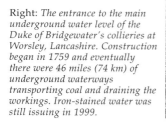

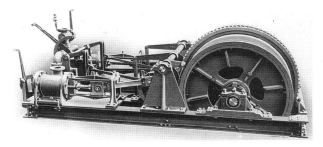

An underground haulage engine that worked on compressed air, with double drum for main and tail ropes.

'empties'. This system worked well but could be used only when the coal was being extracted to the 'rise' of the shafts. As mines developed, coal had to be worked to the 'dip' and for this powered haulage was needed.

The simplest powered system was the single direct rope, where full tubs were hauled up and empties descended by gravity, taking the rope with them. A more productive method was the double rope system, where full tubs ascended and empties descended at the same time, partly counterbalancing the full tubs. Undulating haulage roads needed a different approach. In the 'main and tail' system the main rope hauled the full tubs up ascending gradients while the tail rope plus a

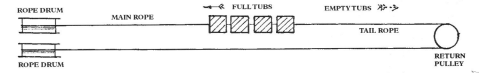

A 'main and tail' haulage system. The tubs were hauled in trains, often twenty-five or more, known as 'gangs' or 'sets'.

brake on the rope drum controlled them on descending gradients. Empty tubs were hauled uphill by the tail rope whilst the main rope controlled them going down. Greatly favoured was the 'endless' haulage system. Tubs were attached at intervals to a continuously moving, endless chain or rope. Speed was low, usually about $1^1/2$ miles per hour (2.5 km/h), but it gave a steady flow of tubs. Endless haulage was equally suited to inclined, undulating or level roads.

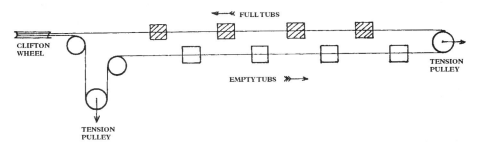

An 'endless rope' haulage system. The tubs were hauled singly or in sets of up to six, each tub or set being spaced out at intervals. The tubs were attached to the rope by friction clip and chain or by a chain lashed on to the rope.

13

Left: *A cross-compound steam haulage engine for installation at the surface with an endless rope passing down the shaft. Built by John Wood & Sons, Wigan.*

Below: *An electrically driven underground 'endless rope' haulage engine.*

Power was at first provided by steam engines located either near the pit bottom or at the surface, with the ropes going down the shaft. Ponies and youths were still needed to provide transport from the working places to where the tubs could be attached to the main haulage system. The introduction of compressed air for power underground meant that small air-driven haulages could be installed quite widely, reducing the use of animals and youths. Mechanisation of coal cutting and the use of coal-face conveyors finally eliminated the need for youths to place tubs at the working places.

Electrically powered rope haulages eventually became widespread but they were still very labour-intensive. A much better coal-haulage system was the conveyor. The troughed belt conveyor could transport large tonnages of coal with little

Underground transport at a colliery in the Wigan district c.1900. A junction of three haulage roadways is shown with 'endless rope' haulage on the left and ponies working the other two roadways.

14

A Ruston & Hornsby class 48 DLG diesel locomotive and man-riding train at New Cumnock Collieries, Ayrshire. Note the roadway supports of straight girders on brick walls.

manpower required. This type was used initially in the main gates carrying coal to a loading point near the main haulage. In the 1950s further development took place with the introduction of conveyor systems to carry coal from the coalface to the shaft bottom. Quite elaborate control systems were needed to ensure that the conveyors stopped and started in sequence. Day-to-day maintenance of conveyors had to be of a high standard. The early years of their extensive use were marred by a number of serious and fatal fires. Regular inspection and fire-resistant belt material largely eliminated these occurrences.

A disadvantage was that conveyors ran in only one direction and were suitable for carrying only coal or 'dirt': a secondary haulage system was required for transporting equipment. Later improvements meant that conveyors could be used for carrying personnel but the difficulty with the transport of equipment remained.

Where it was possible to drive level main haulage roads from the shafts, the introduction of diesel locomotives to haul both mine cars and man-riding cars proved very successful. The locomotives had to have special air, fuel and exhaust systems to make them flameproof. Locomotive haulage is very flexible and can deal with very high tonnages; also it makes the transport of materials and equipment inbye relatively easy. Although some locomotives had been introduced earlier, it was not until after 1945 that they came into their own.

Battery electric locomotives were an alternative to diesel locomotives. Here a battery electric locomotive is shown hauling thirty-five 3 ton capacity mine cars at Bradford Colliery, Manchester.

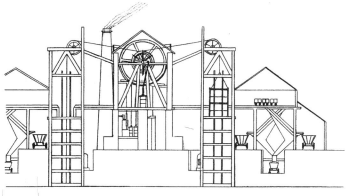

A vertical steam winding engine, winding from two shafts with a single cage in each. This arrangement was in use in the early 1840s and was common in Lancashire.

Winding

For two centuries or more, coal was brought to the surface from the mines by women. They carried it in baskets on their backs up ladders in mine shafts (ladder or 'stair' pits) or up steeply inclined tunnels, known variously as 'drifts', 'day-eyes' or 'in-gaun-ees'. Deeper workings and the need to increase production made necessary some form of mechanical winding system to hoist the coal out of mines. Waterwheels were an effective means of winding but a reliable and plentiful supply of water was essential. Horse-powered gins ('ginnies') usually had to suffice. There was nothing else available until the latter part of the eighteenth century, when engines based on Thomas Newcomen's design were first fitted with crankshafts and winding drums to make crude winding engines. Some collieries used James Watt's engines when they became available but his patent and the shortage of manufacturing capacity discouraged progress. Winding speeds were low and the beam-type engines of Newcomen and Watt were cumbersome. The coal was wound up the shafts in baskets or 'corves', swinging on the end of winding ropes or chains.

In 1800 Phineas Crowther patented an engine with a vertical steam cylinder which drove an overhead crankshaft directly, dispensing with the beam of Newcomen and Watt. It was relatively fast running and became a popular type of winding engine in

Headgear and winding-engine house of the former Bestwood Colliery No. 2 Pit, Nottinghamshire, now preserved. The shaft was completed in December 1875 to the Top Hard seam at a depth of 412 yards (377 metres) and was 13 feet 6 inches (4.1 metres) in diameter. In the engine house is a twin-cylinder vertical steam engine built by R., J. & E. Coupe of Wigan. Commissioned in 1876, it worked until the colliery closed in 1967.

Left: *A nineteenth-century twin-cylinder horizontal winding engine, 36 inches bore by 72 inches stroke (914 mm by 1829 mm), with parallel winding drum 20 feet in diameter by 8 feet wide (6.1 metres by 2.4 metres). Built by Thornewill & Warham, Burton on Trent.*

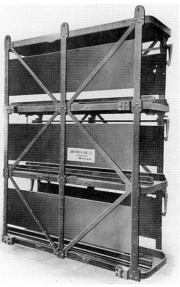

Right: *A three-deck cage for winding coal tubs and men. When winding men, temporary folding gates were fitted. In earlier years men were wound without gates.*

north-east England, the home of its inventor. Although capable of handling relatively large tonnages of coal, it did not find much favour elsewhere. It was not until the mid nineteenth century that fast winding was generally adopted. From the 1850s winding engines with horizontal cylinders and crankshafts on the same axis rapidly gained favour and developed into powerful and fast machines.

With faster winding speed, unguided corves were not practical. Therefore, tubs were wound up in cages instead, guided by wooden rods fixed in the shaft. Later, steel-wire guide ropes, weighted at the bottom, came into use. These gave a smoother ride, so winding could be even faster. Speeds of 90 feet per second (27 metres per second) could be attained in deep shafts.

A nineteenth-century timber headgear in use at Ellerbeck Colliery, Coppull, Lancashire, in 1952. Note the crude steps up one of the legs for access to the pulley bearings.

17

Women working on the pit bank or 'brow' at Moss Hall Arley Pit, Wigan, c.1905. Note the wooden tubs. Women continued to be employed on the surface in Lancashire until the mid 1950s.

At first ordinary ropes and iron chains were used for winding but neither of these was suitable for fast winding or heavy loads. Iron-wire ropes were much better and eventually steel-wire ropes were universally used. Early wire winding ropes were flat and coiled upon themselves on a reel. As manufacturing improved, it was possible to use round ropes that wound on and off a drum.

Early in the twentieth century several large colliery companies introduced electric winding engines but they had to build their own power stations to supply them with electricity. When public electricity supplies became available the use of electric winding engines increased and now electric winding is used throughout Britain's collieries. Many of them are very powerful – 3000 kilowatts and more. Nevertheless, some steam winding engines survived into the 1980s.

In 1877 the first Koepe winding system was installed in Germany. Instead of ropes coiling on and off a drum, a single rope was used, passing partially around a large wheel with shaped wooden blocks fitted on the circumference. The friction between the rope and the wheel was sufficient to operate the cages in the shaft. A later development was the use of up to four ropes of smaller diameter passing around

Left: Metal headgears were being made before 1880 but timber was in general use until the Coal Mines Act of 1911 made the use of timber for new headgears illegal. This headgear of steel was made in the early 1900s by Head, Wrightson & Co Ltd.

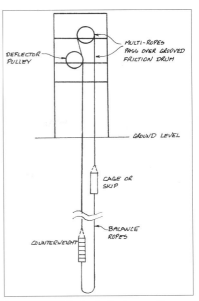

A multi-rope Koepe winding system with tower-mounted winding engine. Frequently a single cage is used together with a counterweight to assist in keeping the rope tensions constant.

friction grooves on a drum. The drum could be of smaller diameter than a single wheel. Multi-rope friction winding engines were usually built into a tower directly above the mine shaft.

Although widely adopted in Germany, there were few Koepe winders in Britain until the 1950s. Bestwood Colliery in Nottinghamshire was one of the first to install a steam Koepe winding engine in 1881. The first electric Koepe winding engine in Britain was installed at Murton Colliery, Northumberland, in 1923. With Koepe electric winding engines there began a move away from fast winding speeds to much lower speeds but heavier loads.

As the use of high-capacity mine cars increased, replacing the small tubs, highly

Left: *A single-rope Koepe electric winding engine powered by two high-speed direct-current motors driving through reduction gearing. Built by Metropolitan-Vickers in the early 1950s.*

Right: *The winding tower at Castlebridge Colliery in Clackmannan, part of the Longannet mine complex that straddles the Fife–Clackmannan border underground. The colliery is carefully screened by trees planted when it was brought into production in the early 1980s.*

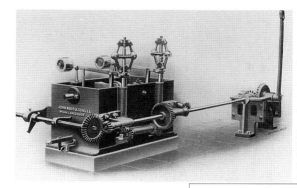

Left: A 'Visor' overwind/overspeed controller for steam winding engines, first applied in 1887 and finally outclassed in the 1930s by increasingly stringent legislation.

Below: An Ormerod detaching hook, showing: A, the hook entering the bell fixed in the headgear on overwind; B, the inner plate striking the bell, shearing the copper pin; the winding rope is released, the hook engages the bell to hold the cage; and C, the winding rope temporarily re-attached to the hook to lower the cage to safety.

mechanised handling systems were installed at pit top and bottom in order to speed up operations. With faster handling and the high coal capacity of the mine cars, greater tonnages could be wound in the working day. An alternative system was skip winding, a skip being a tall, thin, steel box. Coal was tipped into an underground bunker, from which the skips were automatically loaded. Similar arrangements for unloading were provided at the surface. A disadvantage with this system was the break-

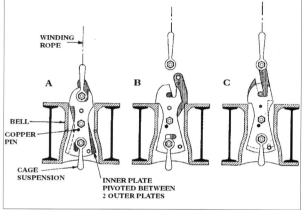

age of coal, and the ensuing dust, but skips could be installed in old, small-diameter shafts to increase winding capacity.

Several serious accidents and fatalities occurred as a result of winding engines failing to stop and the cages going beyond the normal limits of travel. The first device successfully to prevent overwinding was Bertram's 'Visor' of 1887. A purely mechanical device, it shut off steam to the winding engine and applied the brakes if the cages approached the end of their travel at too fast a speed. It did the same should the speed exceed set limits anywhere in the shaft. Other devices followed, some using hydraulic and pneumatic mechanisms. Legislation was introduced in 1911, compelling overwind/overspeed controllers to be fitted to winding engines. Improvements were made as legislation became progressively stricter. The latest controllers continuously monitor speed by electronic means.

To cover any failure of the overwind/overspeed controller, legislation also required a detaching hook to be fitted to the winding ropes: if the ascending cage overshoots, the detaching hook enters a bell that causes the winding rope to be released and also holds the cage. This device does nothing, however, for the descending cage. Koepe winders are provided with buffer stops that arrest the cage and cause the winding rope to slip in the friction groove.

From the mid 1960s many shafts were replaced by long straight drifts even at quite deep mines. The drifts were angled at about fifteen degrees from the horizontal and were termed 'walkable'. Coal was brought right to the surface by conveyors. Manpower requirements were low and, because the drifts were walkable, safety regulations were less onerous than for shafts.

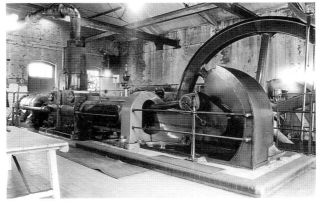

A cross-compound horizontal two-stage air compressor, rated at 5000 cubic feet (140 cubic metres) per minute, made by Walker Brothers of Wigan in 1912. In service at Sutton Manor Colliery, Lancashire, in 1977.

Power

The first successful application of mechanical power in coal mining was the Newcomen pumping engine of 1712, which was designed and built to pump water out of mines. Thus began a long association of steam power with coal mining which did not end until the 1980s, when the last steam winding engines ceased work.

Although steam engines were used underground, they were not very convenient and underground boilers were a hazard with their fires. Compressed air was first used underground in France in 1845. This was a more convenient and safer way of transmitting power and by the end of the nineteenth century was in extensive use in British mines. The use of compressed air declined from the middle of the twentieth century, being retained mainly for the mechanical handling of tubs and mine cars at pit top and bottom, and in very gassy seams.

The demand for steam in collieries became enormous. In the early days, 'haystack' boilers supplied steam to Newcomen engines, operating at $1^1/2$ pounds per square inch or less (0.1 times barometric pressure). These were superseded by the 'egg-ended' boilers that were introduced in about 1800 and which could operate at a pressure of about 30 pounds per square inch (2 bar). Hundreds were used in collieries and a few survived into the 1950s. Another boiler used widely in collieries was the 'Lancashire' boiler invented by William Fairbairn in Manchester in 1844. Of the thousands that were installed in collieries, some remained in service until the 1980s. Improvements in materials and manufacture meant that working pressure gradually increased from 45 pounds (3 bar) to around 160 pounds per square inch (10.6 bar).

In the early part of the twentieth century some ambitious electrical installations were set up for power and lighting. Britannia Colliery in Monmouthshire, which opened in 1910, was Britain's first all-electric mine. Public electricity supplies were still very new and collieries had to build their own power stations. The danger in mines from electricity was open sparking and arcing, which could ignite methane (or 'firedamp'). Before electricity could be used underground with safety, flameproof enclosures were required for motors and switchgear, together with heavily armoured cables. Good ventilation was also needed to ensure low concentrations of firedamp in the mine atmosphere. Electricity from the public supply was a much more convenient form of power and from the 1930s its use at collieries accelerated. It could power a vast range of machinery, from small pumps of a few kilowatts to winding engines of 3000 kilowatts and more. Strict regulations still apply to ventilation and to the construction and use of electrical equipment underground. In a modern mine it is a very safe form of power and is universally used.

Hazards

Mining is a risky business. In the early days miners could breathe in gas or face sudden flooding. There was also the danger of explosion or of the roof caving in.

VENTILATION

As mine workings became more than mere holes in the ground, foul air became a problem. Insufficient oxygen and inflammable and noxious gases combined to make working conditions atrocious. The most dangerous gas in a coal mine is methane (firedamp), which is explosive in concentrations of between 5 and 15 per cent in air. In order for mines to be worked, ventilation was essential. Natural ventilation could sometimes be achieved by linking two shafts underground, but further inducement to make the air flow was usually necessary. An iron basket of burning coal (a 'firelamp') was suspended in one shaft (called the 'upcast'). The firelamp heated the air and induced a flow of fresh air down the other (the 'downcast'). Late in the eighteenth century furnaces were constructed which could create a much greater flow of air. Originally foul air from the mine passed through the furnaces. It was laden with firedamp and highly dangerous. Early in the nineteenth century furnaces began to be arranged so that they took sufficient fresh air for combustion and only discharged hot gases into the upcast shaft to heat the air column. This was a much safer system.

Underground the ventilation was at first 'coursed', passing from the downcast shaft successively through the working areas to the upcast shaft. This meant that the last workings received highly contaminated air and conditions were very bad. Gradually a system of dividing the working areas into 'districts' evolved, each district receiving air direct from the downcast shaft. This made working conditions much better. With either system of ventilation, where access was needed between intake and return airways, airlocks with doors were necessary to avoid short circuiting

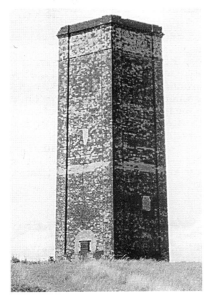

the ventilation. Until 1842 very young children were often employed for very long hours to open and close the doors as tubs came along.

Towards the middle of the nineteenth century, mechanical ventilation was being investigated. Various devices were tried but the only practical means was a centrifugal fan invented by Monsieur Guibal in 1862. This consisted of eight or more rectangular, flat blades that leaned backwards and rotated inside a casing. Air from the mine was drawn into the centre of the fan and was discharged from the blade tips. The blades pushed the air out of the casing into a chimney which tapered outwards, called an *évasée*. Guibal fans were gradually introduced at British collieries. At large collieries the fans could be 50 feet (15.2 metres) in diameter by 12 feet (3.7 metres) wide and were capable of circulating 500,000 cubic feet (14,170 cubic metres) of air through the mine per minute. Improvements were subsequently

The furnace ventilation-shaft chimney, Haigh and Aspull Collieries, near Wigan. It is now preserved as an ancient monument.

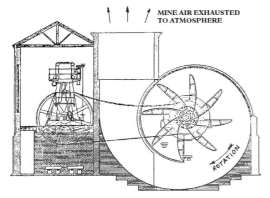

Left: A Walker Brothers backward-bladed centrifugal fan driven by an inverted vertical compound steam engine. A similar fan is preserved at Wigan Pier Heritage Centre.

Below: Side view of a Waddle Patent Fan of the mid 1880s, with steam-engine drive. A more modern example with electric drive can be seen at the National Coal Mining Museum, Caphouse Colliery, near Wakefield.

ROTATION

made by Cockson and by Walker Brothers. The Walker fan had curved blades that leaned backwards and was highly successful. Many remained in use until the mid 1950s.

The multi-vane fan, developed early in the twentieth century, had a large number of forward-curved blades. It was smaller in diameter and ran faster than the backward-bladed fans. It was very successful and a large number were made by Messrs Davidson of Belfast as their 'Sirocco' fan.

The Waddle Patent Fan was completely different: it had fully en-

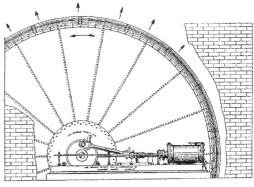

MINE AIR EXHAUSTED TO ATMOSPHERE
AROUND PERIPHERY OF FAN

closed blades and ran in the open. Mine air was drawn into the centre and was discharged freely into the atmosphere around the periphery.

All these fans were known as 'radial-flow' fans as the air entered at the centre and moved outwards to be discharged at the periphery. Later, when aircraft technology was applied to fan design, the outcome was the 'axial-flow' fan, which worked on a similar principle to an aircraft propeller. The propeller blades rotating within a casing act as a screw, pulling a column of air in at the front and pushing it out at the rear. The axial-flow fan is efficient and, although of relatively small size, can deal with large quantities of air. This is the type of fan now generally in use.

Fans, together with larger underground roadways that do not impede air flow, have led to great improvements in ventilation. The resulting dilution of firedamp in the mine atmosphere enabled electricity for power and lighting to be safely introduced.

WATER

Water is often encountered in deep excavations. Rain percolates through surface deposits above the rock and finds its way into faults, fissures and crevices. Some rocks, for example the New Red Sandstones, act like gigantic sponges and absorb huge quantities of water. In the early days of shallow coal workings, natural drainage to watercourses could be relied on to keep the water level down. Deeper workings led to greater problems with water drainage. In some areas long tunnels

A Newcomen-type pumping engine preserved at Dartmouth.

called adits or soughs were driven so that water could flow away to a river or stream. Eventually pumping was needed. As early as 1556 Georgius Agricola was describing pumps for mine drainage, albeit metal mines. His pumps were worked by waterwheels, animals or men. With increasing depths other sources of power were needed.

Thomas Newcomen solved the immediate problem with his atmospheric pumping engine, which was erected at a colliery near Dudley Castle in the West Midlands in 1712. Atmospheric pressure pushed a piston under which a vacuum had been created by condensing steam. A rocking beam transmitted the motion of the piston to a pump rod which went down the mine shaft and drove a pump at the bottom. The large engine at the surface that drove pumps in the mine shaft became a feature of collieries for two centuries. Towards the end of the nineteenth century some collieries installed steam-driven pumps underground near the bottom of the shaft. Where the flow of water into the mine was low, or in an emergency, some collieries used tanks fitted under the cages to lift water. Usually the winding of water was done at night.

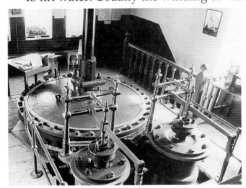

Drainage of remote parts of underground workings could still be a problem. This was first solved by the increasing use of compressed air, which could be piped to small pumps. These delivered water to a 'lodge' at the shaft bottom which was drained by the main pump. The development of the electrical multi-stage centrifugal pump in the early years of the twentieth century provided the best solution for draining mine water. These pumps were small in size relative to the power they developed and could be used anywhere, either as local pumps or as main drainage pumps.

Above: *The cylinder, 70 inches bore by 12 feet stroke (178 cm by 366 cm), of a Cornish steam pumping engine at Prestongrange Colliery, East Lothian. It was built by J. E. Mare of Plymouth Foundry in 1853 and worked until 1954.*

Right: *A portable 3 kilowatt electrically driven triple ram pump for draining workings at the bottom of the 'dip'. Made by John Wood & Sons in the early 1920s.*

A six-stage centrifugal pump powered by a 205 horsepower (152 kilowatt) electric motor, made by Harland Engineering, Alloa, now part of Weir Pumps, Glasgow. This pump could deliver 550 gallons of water per minute (42 litres per second) to a height of 850 feet (259 metres).

Water in disused workings is a great danger. Many lives have been lost by water breaking into working mines from adjacent abandoned pits. Where old workings are being approached, legislation requires boreholes to be driven in advance to act as probes for water. Often abandoned collieries had to be kept open purely to pump water that would otherwise enter the working mines. This was difficult where the old mines had steam-driven pumps. In 1943 a fully submersible, electrically driven pump was installed by the South Yorkshire Mines Drainage Board. This was the forerunner of many similar installations. Suspended in a mine shaft, the submersible pump could be controlled automatically, stopping and starting according to the water level, and could operate for long periods completely unattended.

During the last quarter of the twentieth century a large number of collieries closed and pumping ceased. In many areas ground water levels have risen, flooding former workings and causing subsidence at the surface. There have also been cases of polluted mine water discharging into watercourses. These problems are being carefully investigated but are far from being resolved.

PRECAUTIONS AGAINST EXPLOSION

Until well into the nineteenth century the only safety precaution in coal mines was carried out by the 'fireman'. Clad in wet sacks and carrying a candle on a pole, he was the first one into the mine. He would crawl along the floor, igniting firedamp where it accumulated naturally near the roof. Candles were used to illuminate the working places, leading to frequent explosions, injuries and deaths.

Sir Humphry Davy and George Stephenson both devised safety oil lamps in 1815 where the flame

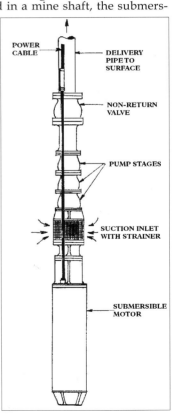

A submersible multi-stage centrifugal pump as used in mine shafts. The pump is suspended from the rising delivery main. Each stage contains an impeller which can lift water approximately 150 feet (45 metres). A three-stage pump can lift water to about 450 feet (135 metres). To raise water to higher levels, more stages are added and a larger motor provided.

25

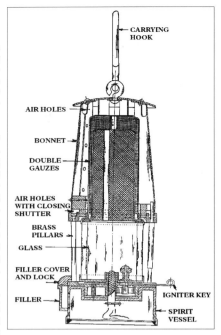

AIR HOLES
BONNET
DOUBLE GAUZES
AIR HOLES WITH CLOSING SHUTTER
BRASS PILLARS
GLASS
FILLER COVER AND LOCK
FILLER

CARRYING HOOK

IGNITER KEY
SPIRIT VESSEL

A colliery official's flame safety lamp with re-igniter as required by law. If they went out, workmen's lamps had to be re-ignited with a separate electric spark igniter at a designated relighting station. Battery electric safety lamps replaced flame lamps for general use from the 1930s, but they could not detect firedamp. A proportion of miners were therefore designated to carry flame lamps.

was enclosed in a gauze to prevent flame transmission. As the illumination they gave was poor, miners were greatly tempted to carry on using candles. Gradual improvements were made to increase brightness, and eventually it became law to use only safety lamps for lighting. They are excellent firedamp detectors, and although electronic detectors are now used, flame safety lamps are an essential back-up device. With a turned-down flame, firedamp can be seen burning above the flame as a 'cap'. The height and shape of this cap give a good indication of the amount of firedamp present in the mine atmosphere.

Shot-firing, sparks from coal-cutter picks, electrical faults and overheated machinery can all cause ignitions. It was discovered that even the aluminium foil wrapping round the tobacco miners took with them to chew could be a source of sparking. Some of the worst explosions were in the early twentieth century. At that time it was only just being realised that a firedamp explosion could trigger a gigantic coal-dust explosion. Hundreds of miners died not only in the initial explosions themselves but also in the ensuing 'afterdamp', which was heavily laden with carbon monoxide. Limestone dust, liberally applied to the floor, sides and roof of roadways, was found to inhibit coal-dust explosions.

It became law in 1911 to establish teams of specially trained rescue men at collieries and also at central rescue stations. An essential part of the rescue team was a canary. Highly sensitive to carbon monoxide, these birds were the only means of detecting this deadly gas until the development of electronic detectors. If the canary put its head under its wing, the men would know that there was carbon monoxide present. If the concentration increased, the bird would fall off its perch. The use of canaries was phased out in the early 1990s. To assist their escape, all miners now carry a 'self rescuer', which is a compact and effective short-term breathing apparatus.

Some major colliery explosions

Year	Colliery	Number of deaths
1866	Oaks Colliery, Yorkshire	361
1885	Clifton Hall Colliery, Lancashire	178
1910	Hulton Collieries, Pretoria Pit, Lancashire	344
1913	Universal Colliery, Senghenydd, South Wales	439 (Britain's worst mining disaster)
1934	Gresford Colliery, Wrexham	265
1947	William Pit, Whitehaven, Cumbria	104

Women working at an old fixed bar screen at a colliery in the Wigan district c.1900.

Preparing the coal for sale

The old miners were forbidden to send small coal and stone (dirt) to the surface on pain of a fine or dismissal. It had to be left underground. What was regarded as 'small' depended on the whim of the mine owner. Many customers did not want to buy small coal ('slack'). To prepare the coal for sale, it was tipped on to a grid of parallel iron bars. What went through was slack, and what remained on top was lumps. The largest lumps were picked off to be sold separately at the highest price. The remaining, smaller pieces were sold as 'cobbles'.

As the intensity of mining increased it was inevitable that stone and shale would arrive at the surface mixed with the coal. Moving belts were installed on to which

Left: *Women workers at the extensive screening plant of Douglas Bank Colliery, Wigan, in the early 1900s.*

Right: *The 'picking belts' at Manton Colliery, Nottingham-shire, in the early 1900s, with workmen picking off the dirt – a colliery scene which was little changed for some fifty years. In Lancashire this work was carried out mainly by women.*

27

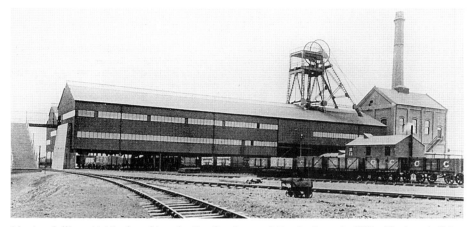

Manton Colliery, Nottinghamshire, shortly after its completion in the early 1900s. The long building (under which the railway wagons are passing) houses the screens.

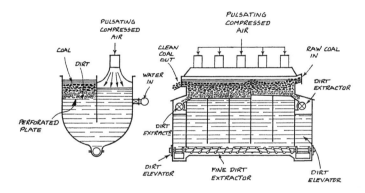

A jig-type coal washer. This type of machine could deal with lumps of coal measuring from 6 inches across to half an inch (150 mm to 12 mm).

the coal was tipped; the dirt was picked off by hand, and the largest pieces of coal could also be pulled off at this stage. From the end of the picking belts, the coal passed on to a series of shaking screens (like giant sieves) which graded the coal into sizes. The different sizes were loaded into separate railway wagons.

To improve the quality of small coal and make it more marketable, coal washers were being used by the mid 1860s. It was near the end of the century, however, before this system became widespread. By the mid twentieth century, coal washing had developed into a highly scientific process. Clean coal is quite light and will float in a tank of water that is being 'jigged' up and down or upon a water-based dense medium. The floating coal can then be skimmed off. Coal with dirt in it sinks and can also be removed from the tank. By crushing the dirty coal, the dirt and coal can be partially separated. The mixture can then be rewashed in a separate tank. Finally, the very finest particles of coal can be floated on froth, skimmed off and dried.

Coal mining today

The peak of coal production in 1913, amounting to 287 million tons, was achieved by 1.1 million miners working at 3024 mines. In 1947, when the mines were nationalised, 187.5 million tons were produced by 703,900 miners at 1296 mines. During the last quarter of the twentieth century deep mining of coal suffered a tremendous decline. In 1998 output was down to 25 million tons from just eighteen major mines.

The Second World War led to the introduction of large-scale opencast mining, which is virtually quarrying, at a time when coal was in great demand. Huge excavating machines imported from the United States removed surface deposits above the coal seams, which were then extracted by mechanical shovels. The quality of opencast coal is inferior to deep-mined coal but is acceptable for some markets, in particular the electricity generating stations. Productivity is high and safety easier to achieve than in deep mining. Although disruption to the landscape is severe it is temporary. It was thought that opencast mining would be short-lived, as shallow coal deposits were finite and often affected by old mining. However, machinery has constantly improved so that coal more than 300 feet (100 metres) deep can be reached. In some areas, since the closure of deep mines, opencast workings can be affected by rising ground-water levels, making coal extraction uneconomic or impractical.

A market for coal in Britain is likely for many years, especially for the generation of electricity (which consumed 48 million tons of coal in 1998). In 1998 British coal production was 41.4 million tons, of which 15 million tons was obtained by opencast mining and 1.4 million tons was recovered from dirt tips and other dumps. The total consumption was 63 million tons, of which 2.2 million tons was for domestic use. The balance between production and consumption was made up by imports, which are gradually increasing.

An electrically driven axial-flow propeller fan made in 1950 for Standish Hall drift mine, near Wigan.

Some mining terms

Adit: a tunnel into a mine to drain water (also known as a sough).

Afterdamp: the gases present in the mine atmosphere following an explosion; contains a large proportion of carbon monoxide.

Airlock: a structure to prevent short-circuiting of ventilation air; has doors for access which are normally shut.

Banksman: the person in charge of the cages at the top of the mine shafts.

Blackdamp: an irrespirable mixture of carbon dioxide and nitrogen.

Chock: a roof support built from interlaced hardwood blocks.

Dip: the downward slope or tilt of coal seams (opposite of *Rise*).

Dirt: stone and shale.

Downcast: the shaft taking fresh air into the mine (opposite of *Upcast*).

Drawing off: removing roof supports, i.e. props and chocks.

Drift: a tunnel that slopes down from the surface.

Dykes (and Sills): solidified volcanic magma passing through a coal seam.

Fault: a fracture in the rocks that form the earth's crust, causing displacement of the rock beds and coal seams.

Firedamp: flammable and explosive gas consisting mostly of methane.

Firehole: the colliery boiler plant.

Fireman: the person responsible for the safety of a part or 'district' of a mine, more properly called a deputy.

Gate or Gate road: a tunnel serving a longwall face which is extended as the face advances.

Heading: a dead–end tunnel usually driven for exploration or development.

Hole out: a deep cut or slot made by miners.

Inbye: going away from the shafts towards the coalface (opposite of *Outbye*).

Jib: the arm fitted to a coal-cutting machine around which the coal-cutting chain runs.

Longwall face: a working face of considerable length in a coal seam, from which coal is cut or sliced off from end to end.

Nogs: hardwood blocks, slightly wedge-shaped, driven into the slot made by the coal-cutting machine to hold up the coal.

Onsetter: the person in charge of the cages at the bottom of the mine shaft.

Outbye: going towards the shafts (opposite of *Inbye*).

Pillar: a block of solid coal left unworked in order to support the roof.

Rise: the upward slope or tilt of coal seams (opposite of *Dip*).

Shaft pillar: the area around the shafts where the coal is left unworked to prevent ground movement.

Sills: see *Dykes*.

Sough: (pronounced 'suff') a drainage tunnel connecting mine workings with a watercourse in old mining practice.

Sprag: a short prop made of wood.

Stinkdamp: hydrogen sulphide gas.

Strike: an imaginary line at right angles to the dip; the strike is always horizontal.

Sylvester: a ratchet and chain device for drawing off roof supports from a safe distance.

Upcast: the shaft carrying foul or return air out of the mine (opposite of *Downcast*).

Washout: the part of a coal seam that has been washed away by a prehistoric river.

Waste: the area from which a coal seam has been completely extracted; also known as the *Goaf* or *Gob*.

Whitedamp: carbon monoxide gas, highly poisonous.

Winder: the person in charge of the winding engine.

Further reading

Anderson, D. *The Orrell Coalfield, Lancashire 1740-1850*. Moorland Publishing, Hartington, 1975.

Anderson, D. *Coal: A Pictorial History of the British Coal Industry*. David & Charles, 1982.

Anderson, D. *Blundell's Collieries 1776-1966*. Published by the author, Wigan, 1986.

Anderson, D., France, A. A., and Lane, J. *The Standish Collieries 1635-1963*. Published by D. Anderson, Wigan, 1984.

Anderson, D., and France, A. A. *Wigan Coal and Iron*. Smith's Books, Wigan, 1994.

Banks, A. G., and Schofield, R. B. *Brindley at Wet Earth Colliery*. David & Charles, 1968.

Devlin, R., and Fancy, H. *The Most Dangerous Pit in the Kingdom*. The Friends of Whitehaven Museum, 1997.

Down, C. G., and Warrington, A. J. *The History of the Somerset Coalfield*. David & Charles, 1972.

Hayes, G. *Collieries in the Manchester Coalfields*. De Archaeologische Pers, Eindhoven, 1987.

Hutton, G. *Mining: Ayrshire's Lost Industry*. Stenlake Publishing, Cumnock, 1996.

Hutton, G. *Lanarkshire's Mining Legacy*. Stenlake Publishing, Cumnock, 1997.

Hutton, G. *Mining the Lothians*. Stenlake Publishing, Ochiltree, 1998.

Owen, J. S. *Coal Mining at Brora 1529-1974*. Highland Libraries, Inverness, 1995.

The 'pit bank' at Ellerbeck Colliery, Lancashire, c.1952. Two empty tubs are in the cage ready to descend, and two full tubs have just been taken out.

Places to visit

Intending visitors are advised to check the times of opening before travelling.

FORMER COLLIERY SITES

Astley Green Colliery Museum, Higher Green Lane, Astley, Tyldesley, Greater Manchester. Telephone: 01772 431937.

Bestwood Colliery No. 2 Pit, Bestwood Country Park, Nottingham.

Big Pit Mining Museum, Blaenavon, Torfaen NP4 9XP. Telephone: 01495 790311. Website: www.citypages.co.uk/wales/np/bigpit

Cefn Coed Colliery Museum, Neath Road, Crynant, Neath SA10 8SN. Telephone: 01639 750556.

Elsecar Heritage Centre, Wath Road, Elsecar, Barnsley, South Yorkshire S74 8HJ. Telephone: 01226 740203.

Haig Colliery Mining Museum, Solway Road, Kells, Whitehaven, Cumbria CA28 9BG. Telephone: 01946 599949.

National Coal Mining Museum for England, Caphouse Colliery, New Road, Overton, Wakefield, West Yorkshire WF4 4RH. Telephone: 01924 848806. Website: www.ncm.org.uk

Prestongrange Industrial Heritage Museum, Morison's Haven, near Prestonpans, East Lothian EH32 9SA. Telephone: 01620 828203. Website: www.elothian-museums.demon.co.uk

Rhondda Heritage Park, Lewis Merthyr Colliery, Coed Cae Road, Trehafod, Rhondda CF37 7NF. Telephone: 01443 682036. Website: www.netwales.co.uk/rhondda-heritage

Scottish Mining Museum Trust, Lady Victoria Colliery, Newtongrange, Midlothian EH22 4QN. Telephone: 0131 663 7519. Website: www.scottishminingmuseum.com

Snibston Discovery Park, Ashby Road, Coalville, Leicestershire LE67 3LN. Telephone: 01530 510851.

Washington 'F' Pit Industrial Museum, Albany Way, Albany, District 2, Washington, Tyne and Wear. Telephone: 0191 416 7640.

Woodhorn Colliery Museum, Queen Elizabeth II Country Park, Ashington, Northumberland NE63 9YF. Telephone: 01670 856968.

MUSEUMS

Beamish – The North of England Open Air Museum, Beamish, County Durham DH9 0RG. Telephone: 01207 231811. Website: www.merlins.demon.co.uk/beamish

Black Country Living Museum, Tipton Road, Dudley, West Midlands DY1 4SQ. Telephone: 0121 557 9643. Website: www.bclm.co.uk

Derby Industrial Museum, Full Street, Derby DE1 3AR. Telephone: 01332 255308.

Engine House, Mayors Avenue, Dartmouth, Devon TQ6 9YY. Telephone: 01803 834224. Website: www.dartmouth-tourism.org.uk

Ironbridge Gorge Museum Trust, Ironbridge, Telford, Shropshire TF8 7AW. Telephone: 01952 433522. Website: www.vtel.co.uk/igmt

Kidwelly Industrial Museum, Broadford, Kidwelly, Carmarthenshire SA17 4LW. Telephone: 01554 891078.

Lancashire Mining Museum, Buile Hill Park, Eccles Old Road, Salford, Lancashire M6 8GL. Telephone: 0161 736 1832.

Papplewick Pumping Station, off Longdale Lane, Ravenshead, Nottinghamshire NG15 9AJ. Telephone: 0115 963 2938.

Royal Museum of Scotland, Chambers Street, Edinburgh EH1 1JF. Telephone: 0131 225 7534. Website: www.nms.ac.uk

Science Museum, Exhibition Road, South Kensington, London SW7 2DD. Telephone: 020 7938 8000. Website: www.nmsi.ac.uk

South Wales Miners' Museum, Afan Argoed Countryside Centre, Cynonville, Port Talbot SA13 3HG. Telephone: 01639 850564.

Summerlee Heritage Park, Heritage Way, Coatbridge, Lanarkshire ML5 1QD. Telephone: 01236 431261.

Trencherfield Mill – Wigan Pier Heritage Centre, Wigan, Lancashire WN4 4EF. Telephone: 01942 323666.